Farm Animals

And Worksheet

In this farm animals worksheet set includes:
1.Poster farm animals.
2.Picture word farm animals.
3.Match the shadows.
4.Word tracing.
5.How do you see?
6.Count and circle the number.
7.Read and color.
8.Find the same picture .
9.Fill the missing vowels.

By Sarah Oan

Farm Animals

Sheep

Duck

Rooster

Turkey

Goat

Rabbit

Goose

Pig

Dog

Horse

Chicken

Cat

Donkey

Cow

Bull

Picture Word

Sheep

Duck

Rooster

Turkey

Goat

Rabbit

Goose

Pig

Dog

Horse

Chicken

Cat

Donkey

Cow

Bull

NAME:

Match the shadows

Match the shadows

Word tracing

Sheep

Duck

Rooster

Turkey

Goat

Rabbit

Goose

Pig

Dog

Horse

Chicken

Cat

Donkey

Cow

Bull

Word tracing

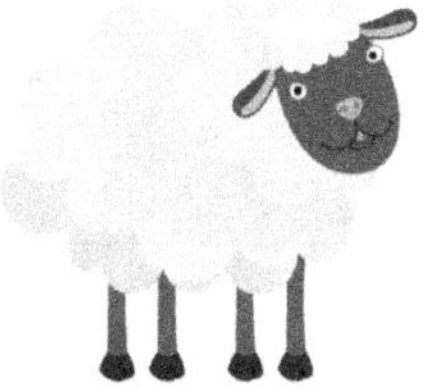

Sheep

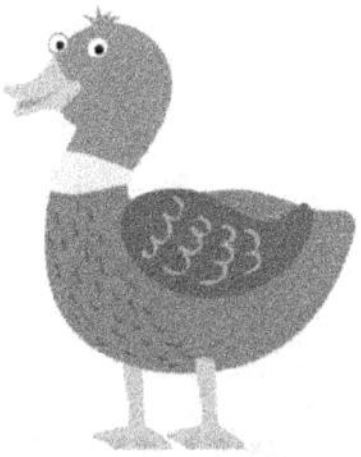

Duck

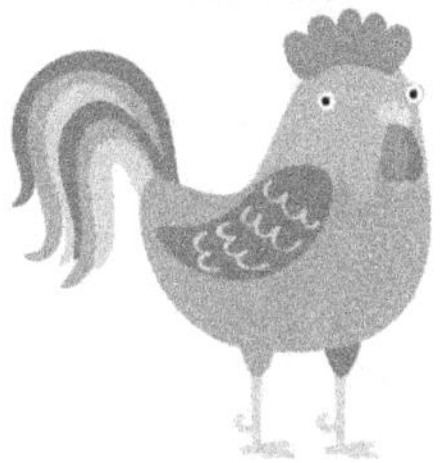

Rooster

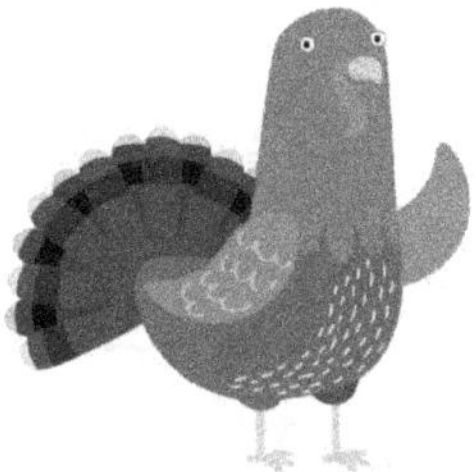

Turkey

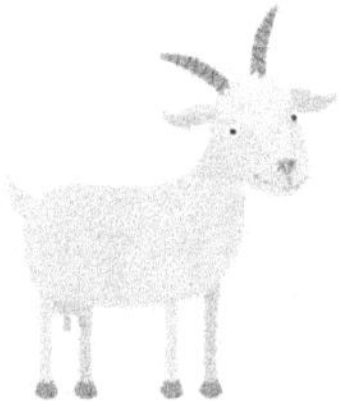

Goat

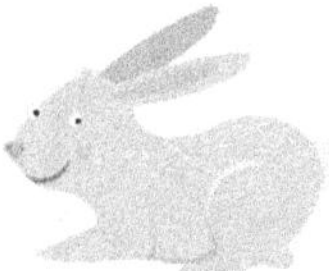

Rabbit

Goose

Word tracing

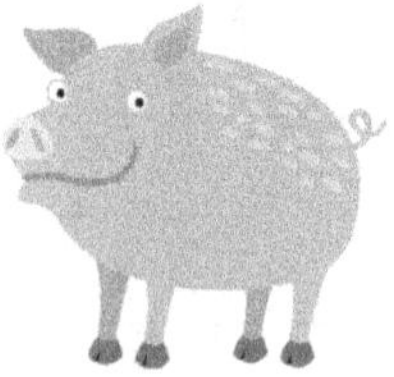

Pig

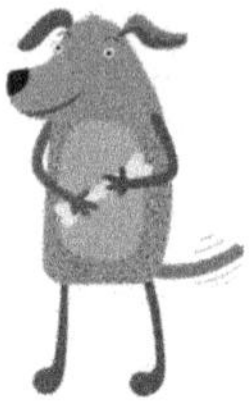

Dog

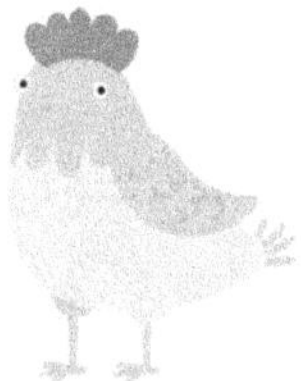

Chicken

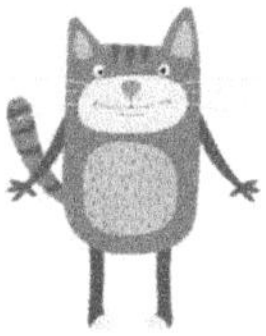

Cat

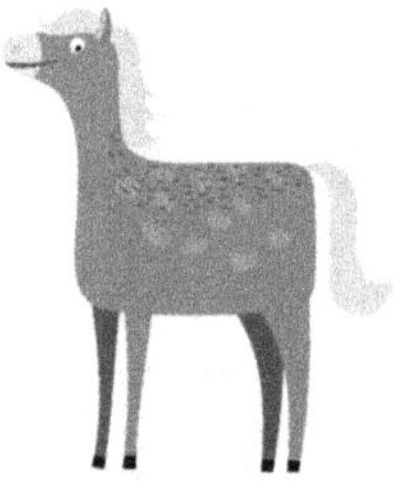

Horse

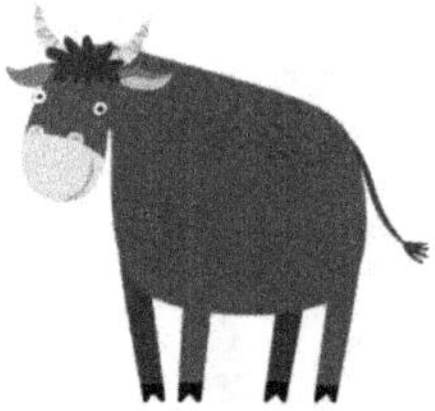

Bull

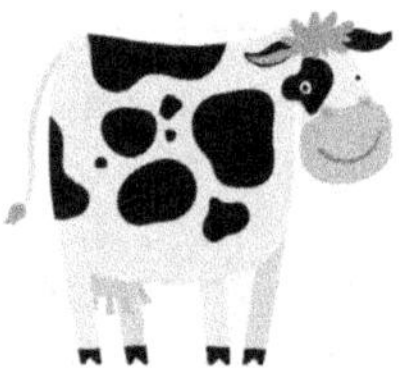

Cow

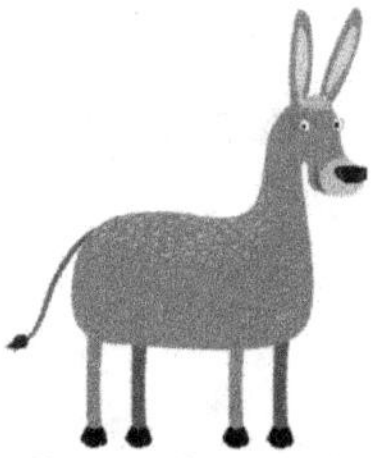

Donkey

How many do you see?

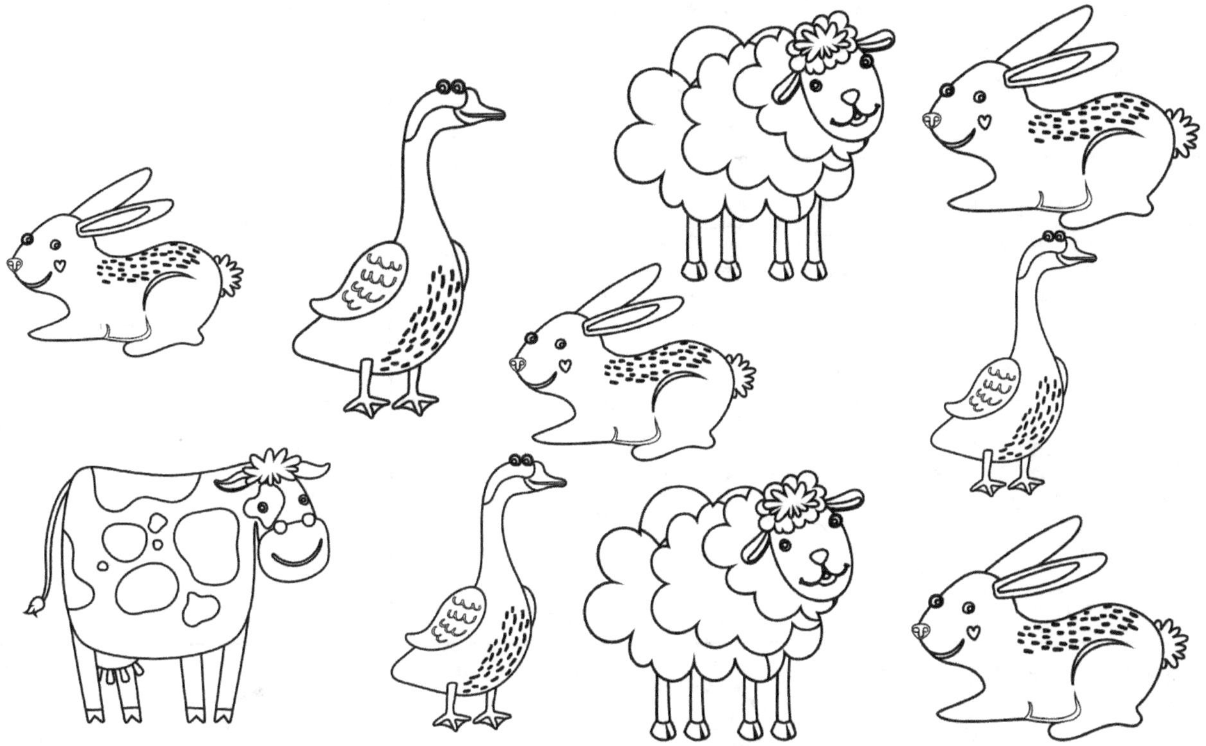

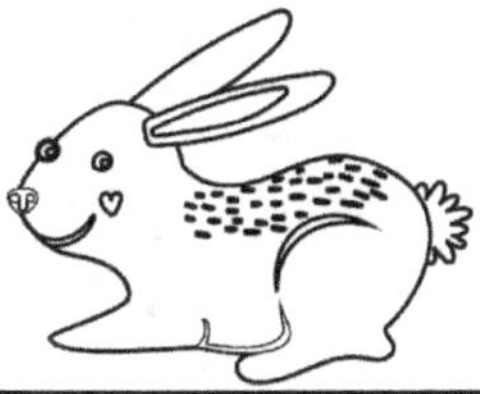	1	2	3	4
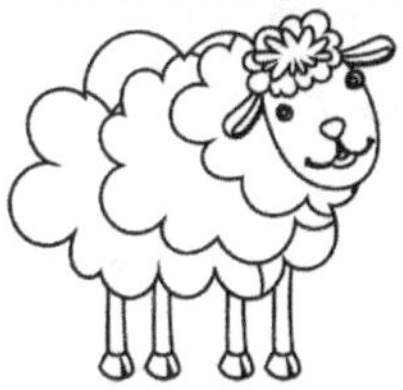	1	2	3	4
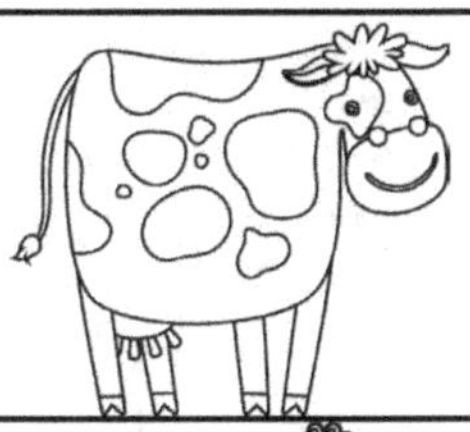	1	2	3	4
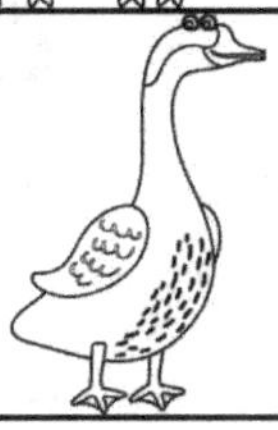	1	2	3	4

NAME:

Count and circle the number

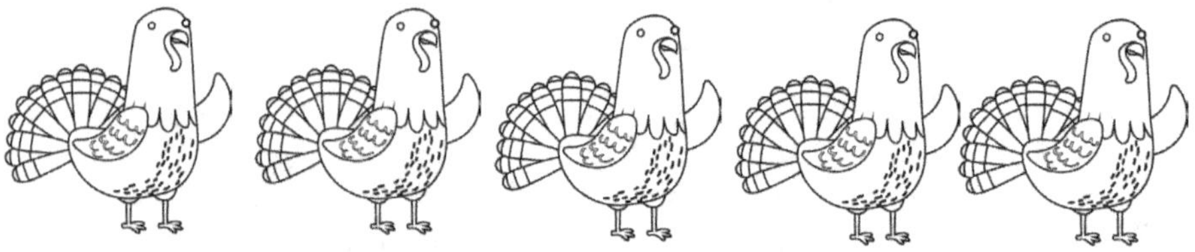	4 5 6
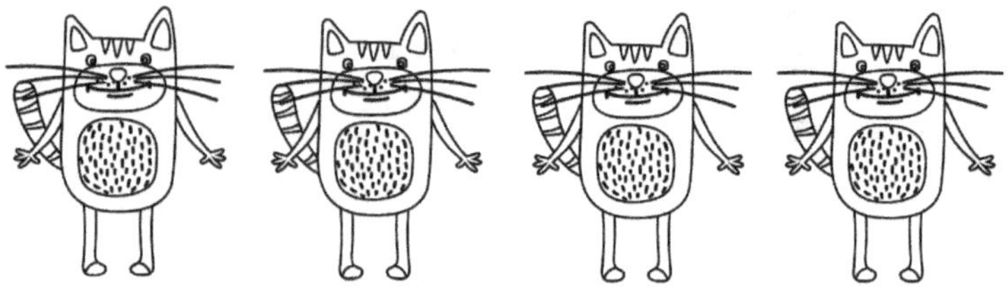	4 5 6
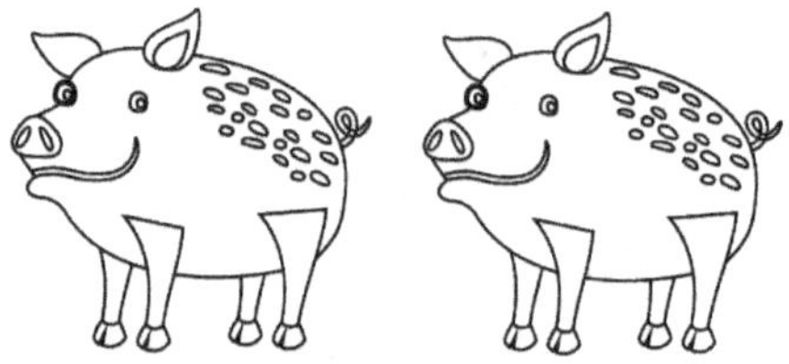	1 2 3
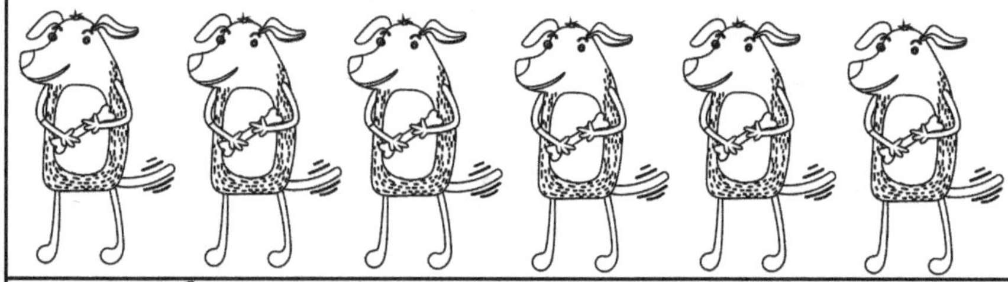	5 6 7
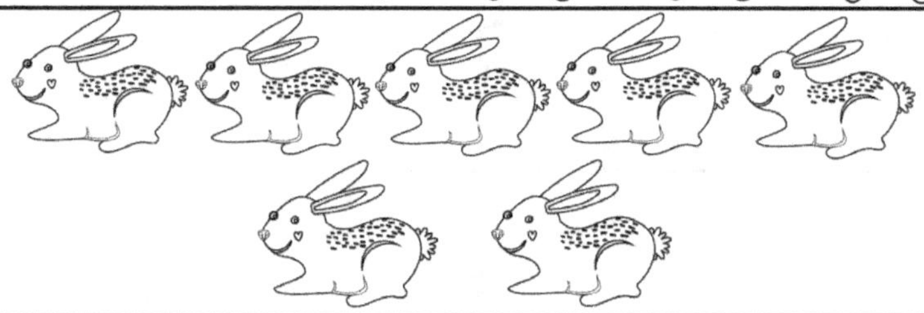	5 6 7
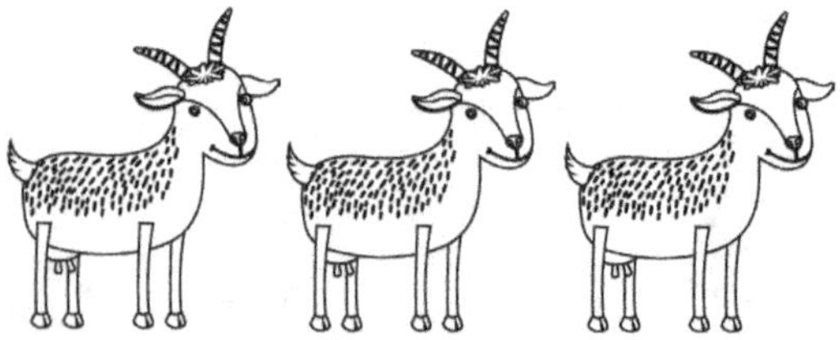	1 2 3
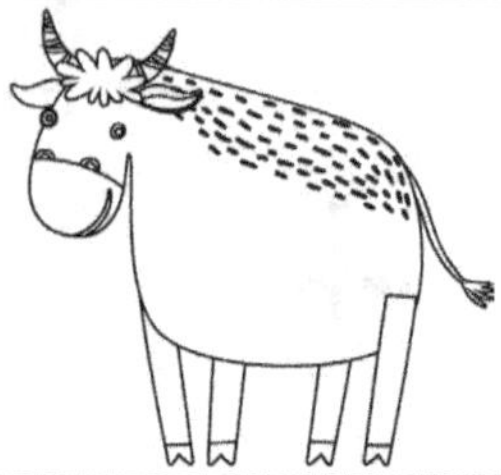	1 2 3

Read And Color

Horse Turkey Donkey

Chicken Goat

Find the same picture

Fill the missing vowels.

 Sh_ _p

 Ch_ck_n

 R__st_r

 C_t

 D_nk_y

 R_bb_t

 D_ck

 P_g

Fill the missing vowels.

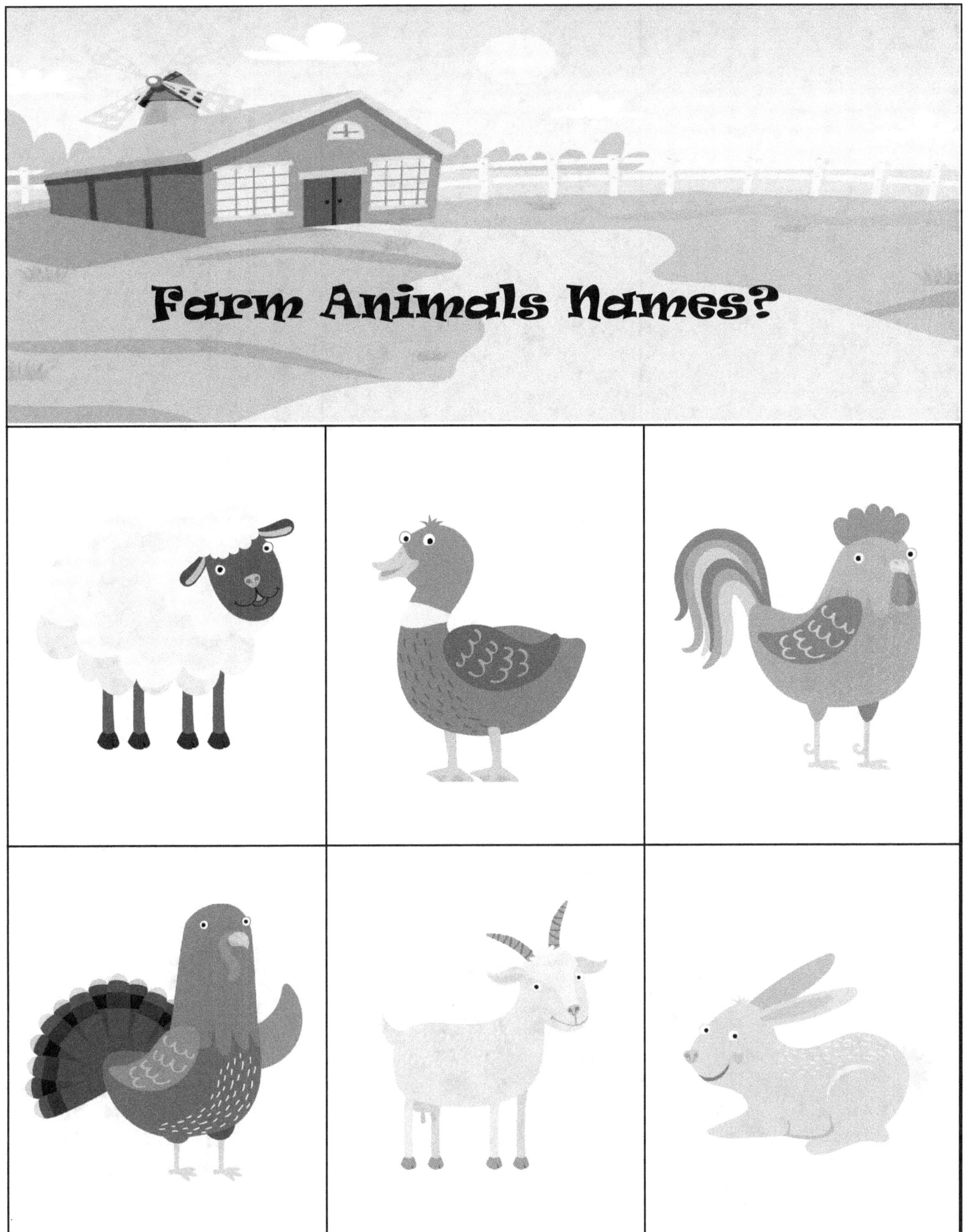

Farm Animals Names?